Do You Really Want a Lizard?

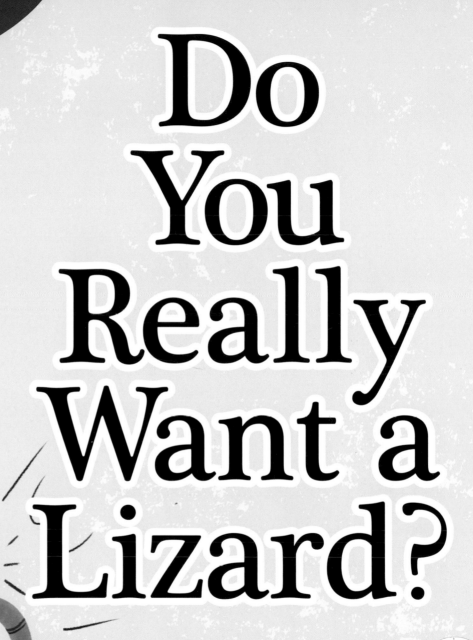

Bridget Heos • Illustrated by Katya Longhi

Amicus Illustrated is published by Amicus
P.O. Box 1329, Mankato, MN 56002
www.amicuspublishing.us

Library of Congress Cataloging-in-Publication Data
Heos, Bridget, author.
 Do you really want a lizard? / by Bridget Heos.
    pages cm. — (Amicus illustrated) (Do you really want a pet?)
 Summary: "Several lizards (and the narrator) teach a young girl the
responsibility—and the joys—of caring for a pet lizard. Includes "Is this pet
right for me?" quiz"— Provided by publisher.
 Audience: K to grade 3.
 Includes bibliographical references.
 ISBN 978-1-60753-750-2 (library binding) — ISBN 978-1-60753-849-3 (ebook)
 1. Lizards as pets—Juvenile literature. I. Longhi, Katya, illustrator. II. Title. III. Series:
Heos, Bridget. Do you really want a pet?
 SF459.L5H46 2016
 639.3'95—dc23   2014033272

Editor   Rebecca Glaser
Designer   Kathleen Petelinsek

Printed in the United States of America at
Corporate Graphics in North Mankato, Minnesota.

10 9 8 7 6 5 4 3 2 1

About the Author

Bridget Heos is the author of more than
70 books for children including *Mustache Baby*
and *Mustache Baby Meets His Match*. Her family
has two pets, an old dog named Ben and a young
cat named Homer. You can find out more about
her at www.authorbridgetheos.com.

About the Illustrator

Katya Longhi was born in southern Italy.
She studied illustration at the Nemo NT
Academy of Digital Arts in Florence. She loves
to create dream worlds with horses, flying
dogs, and princesses in her illustrations.
She currently lives in northern Italy
with her Prince Charming.

So you say you want a lizard. You really, really want a lizard.

But do you *really* want a lizard?

It will need a habitat that is like its home in the wild.

Otherwise ...

. . . it will get lost in your home.
Especially if it's a chameleon!

You'll need a terrarium. (It's like an aquarium but isn't filled with water.) A small lizard's terrarium can fit on a dresser.

A larger lizard, like an iguana, on the other hand . . .

. . . needs a terrarium as big as a bathroom.
You may not have that much space.

But what kind of lizard *do* you want?

Chameleons are beautiful but difficult. They're best for families who have owned lizards before.

Instead, how about . . .

. . . a bearded dragon? They are
calm and cute. And distinguished!

PRESIDENT ABRAHAM LIZARD

Bearded dragons are from the desert. They need sand and dry air. They also like to have a place to hide.

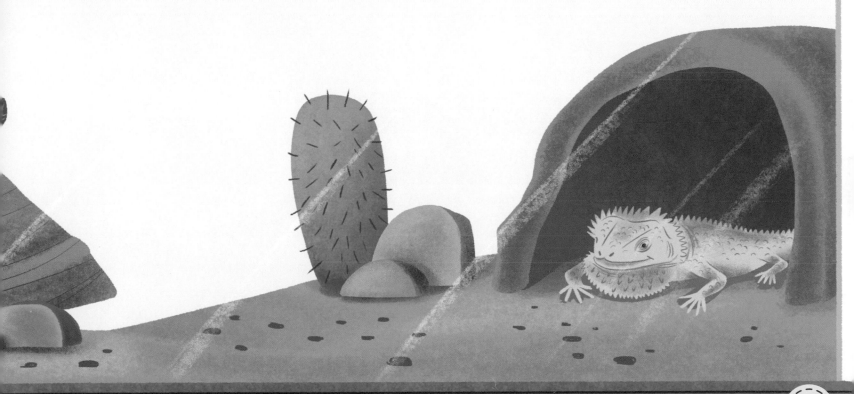

Or how about a gecko? Geckos are from the forest, so they need branches for climbing.

I'm starving!

10

No matter what type you choose, your lizard will need water and food.

And lizard food is . . .

... alive! Most lizards eat live insects, including crickets and mealworms.

Keep your insects in a small plastic cage. Let them climb on empty cardboard tubes. You'll have to feed the insects, too! You can buy cricket chow or feed them fresh foods like greens and potatoes.

In the morning, take out one tube.
Shake it into your lizard's terrarium.

Bearded dragons like vegetables and fruits, too.

Besides food, your lizard needs sunlight to stay healthy. Inside, you'll need special lamps to take the place of the sun. Your lizard will bask under these to warm up.

And finally . . .

. . . even though it's yucky, you'll need to clean the terrarium. Scoop out poop every day. Once a month, throw away the sand.

Then wash the terrarium and bowls with bleach and water.

Add new sand and put everything back.

Uh-oh! Even with the best care, lizards can get sick. If your lizard stops eating, take it to a reptile veterinarian.

19

Now how about some bonding time? Well, lizards don't really like to snuggle. You can talk to your lizard, though. And watch it do cool things.

I love ya, sis, but I'm not a hugger.

So if you're willing to give your
pet food, water, and a good habitat,
then maybe you really do want a lizard.

Now I have a question for the lizard. You say you
want a person. You really, really want a person.
But do you *really*
want a person?

QUIZ

Is this the right pet for me?

Should you get a lizard? Complete this quiz to find out. (Be sure to talk to breeders, rescue groups, or pet store workers, too!)

1. Are you able to keep live insects to feed the lizard?
2. Are you okay with not cuddling with your pet?
3. Can you make sure the terrarium is the right temperature and humidity?

If you answered . . .

a. NO TO NUMBER ONE, but you like reptiles, you might consider a plant-eating turtle instead.
b. NO TO NUMBER TWO, then an animal that likes to cuddle, like a dog or cat, may be better.
c. NO TO THREE, you may like a hamster or guinea pig better.
d. YES TO ALL THREE QUESTIONS, a lizard might be the right pet for you!

Websites

Bearded Dragon Care
www.thebeardeddragon.org/bearded-dragon-care.php
Learn how to care for a bearded dragon.

Bearded Dragons as Pets for Kids
pets.petsmart.com/guides/bearded-dragons/
tips-for-kids.shtml
Read fun facts, care tips, and learn about feeding and
habitats for this popular pet lizard.

Leopard Gecko: Tips for Kids
pets.petsmart.com/guides/leopard-geckos/tips-for-kids.shtml
Read important care tips and fun facts about this spotted
lizard.

Reptile Care for Beginners
www.reptilesmagazine.com/Reptile-Care-For-Beginners/
Reptiles Magazine offers articles about reptile pet care,
choosing a reptile pet, and information for kids who are
getting a lizard for the first time.

Every effort has been made to ensure that these websites are appropriate
for children. However, because of the nature of the Internet, it is impossible
to guarantee that these sites will remain active indefinitely or that their
contents will not be altered.

Read More

Carr, Aaron. *Iguana*. I Love My Pet.
New York: AV2 by Weigl, 2013.

Nevin, Felicia Lowenstein. *Learning
to Care for Reptiles and Amphibians*.
Beginning Pet Care with American
Humane. Berkeley Heights, NJ: Bailey
Books/Enslow, 2011.

Petrie, Kristin. *Chameleons*. Unique
Pets. Minneapolis: ABDO, 2013.

Raum, Elizabeth. *Bearded Dragons*.
Lizards. Mankato, Minn.: Amicus, 2014.

Sssss....